Conquering Anxiety
Strategies to Regain Control

Table of Contents

Chapter 1. Introduction

In this transformative Special Report titled "Conquering Anxiety: Strategies to Regain Control," we traverse the demystifying path of understanding anxiety and learning to regain control over our lives. Navigating through the terrains of personal experiences, expert inputs, and an array of proven techniques, the report serves as a beacon of hope for everyone yearning to liberate themselves from anxiety's shackles. It's anything but technical, and more of an enlightening journey that will bring refreshing positivity into your life. Don't miss out on this vibrant guide—it's not only illuminating but empowering too. Embrace the opportunity to seize back control of your life today—because everybody deserves an anxiety-free life, and it starts with this Special Report.

Chapter 2. Understanding Anxiety: Essential Background

Anxiety is as old as mankind itself, and surprisingly, it's a normal part of living—when in moderation. But when it starts to interfere with everyday functioning, that's when the alarms start ringing. Let's take a comprehensive look at exactly what we're dealing with.

2.1. The Anatomy of Anxiety

Anxiety isn't just a feeling — it's a complex response system. Anxiety triggers our body's "fight-or-flight" response, a primitive survival mechanism designed to alert us to danger and prepare us to either confront or flee from threatening situations.

When this system is activated, the adrenal glands release adrenaline (also known as epinephrine), a hormone that prepares the body for action by increasing heart rate and blood pressure, sharpening the senses, remobilizing energy stores, and enhancing physical performance. It's a brilliant, effective system that significantly aided survival when human beings were hunting and gathering.

Anxiety becomes a problem when this system gets triggered unnecessarily, creating a state of heightened alertness and fear, despite the absence of any genuine threat.

Let's understand anxiety a bit more.

2.2. Normal Anxiety VS Anxiety Disorders

The occasional experience of anxiety, especially in response to specific events or situations, is completely normal. Normal anxiety can be described as temporary worry or fear felt before making an important decision, facing a challenging situation, or participating in a major event. It's a natural reaction to stress, and it usually subsides once the cause of anxiety is resolved.

However, when anxiety becomes chronic or uncontrollable, significantly impacts one's daily life and lasts for more than six months, it is considered an anxiety disorder.

Anxiety disorders are a group of mental health conditions characterized by extreme, debilitating anxiety. They include:

1. Generalized Anxiety Disorder (GAD)

2. Social Anxiety Disorder (Social Phobia)

3. Panic Disorder

4. Obsessive-Compulsive Disorder (OCD)

5. Post-traumatic Stress Disorder (PTSD)

6. Specific Phobias

Each of these disorders has unique symptoms, but excessive, lingering worry and fear are common to all. In fact, statistics indicate that anxiety disorders are the most common mental health disorders, affecting almost 30% of adults at some point in their lives.

2.3. Physical and Psychological Symptoms

Now that we've understood what constitutes an anxiety disorder, let's delve into its various manifestations. Anxiety can produce a wide range of physical and psychological symptoms.

Physical symptoms of anxiety can include:

1. Rapid heartbeat

2. Sweating

3. Trembling or shaking

4. Feeling weak or tired

5. Difficulty breathing

6. Sleep problems

In addition to these physical symptoms, anxiety can also manifest psychologically, leading to symptoms such as:

1. Persistent worry or fear

2. Difficulty concentrating

3. Feeling tense or on edge

4. Expecting the worst

5. Restlessness

Remember, everyone experiences anxiety differently. Some people might experience mostly physical symptoms, like a racing heart and tremors, while others might grapple with psychological symptoms such as constant worry or fear.

2.4. Causes of Anxiety

A combination of factors contributes to anxiety disorders. These can include genetics, brain chemistry, personality, and life events.

Genetics can play a significant role in increasing the chances of developing an anxiety disorder. If an individual has immediate family members with anxiety disorders, they may be at higher risk.

Regarding brain chemistry, neurotransmitters (chemical messengers in the brain) play pivotal roles in controlling feelings and thoughts. When these chemicals are out of balance, it may cause anxiety.

Certain personality types are more prone to anxiety disorders. For instance, people who are perfectionists, easily flustered, shy, or want to control everything may have higher anxiety levels.

Lastly, traumatic life events, such as the death of a loved one, can trigger anxiety disorders. Ongoing stressful events, like job-related stress, may also lead to these conditions.

Chapter 3. In Conclusion

Understanding anxiety sets the foundation for learning to deal with it. Whether you think you suffer from an anxiety disorder or just want to better manage everyday stress, understanding the nature of anxiety and how it manifests can be exceptionally beneficial. The next sections will deep-dive into the ways to conquer anxiety.

Chapter 4. Exploring the Roots of Anxiety

To understand a tree, one must first examine its roots. In this case, we're examining the roots of anxiety, delving into the factors that precipitate these feelings of unease and fear—an investigation that rests its focus on our biological, environmental, and psychological cues.

4.1. Genetic and Biological Factors

Anxiety often runs in families, signifying a genetic precursor. Research indicates that certain genes play a role in developing anxiety disorders. It's fascinating, yet alarming, how a small composition of our bodily code can predetermine our propensity to a state of chronic worry. This, however, is not the sole determiner. The intriguing world of epigenetics shows us how our environment can interact with our genes, switching them "on" or "off."

Biological factors extend beyond our genetic mapping. When we experience anxiety, there's a flurry of activity happening in our brain. The amygdala, our brain's fear center, is in constant communication with the prefrontal cortex, the area responsible for judgment and decision making. When anxiety hits, this communication goes haywire. The amygdala screams danger, while the prefrontal cortex, overwhelmed, fails to rationalize and calm us down. It's a biological frenzy causing our pounding hearts, sweaty palms, and restlessness.

4.2. Environmental Factors

All around us, there are triggers, some conspicuous and others inconspicuous, leading us towards anxiety. Growing up in a chronically stressful, abusive, or deprived environment can significantly increase one's risk of developing an anxiety disorder. Life events, both traumatic and stressful, also play a role. Loss of a loved one, experiencing violence, or prolonged financial stress are potent wellsprings of anxiety.

A subtler form of environmental influence is cultural expectations and societal pressures. The constant demand to conform, excel, and showcase an ever radiant exterior fuels anxiety, particularly among younger populations.

Besides, our modern, hyper-connected world has brought along a unique array of triggers. The omnipresence of news, often negative, can induce anxiety. So can the pressure of maintaining online social personas and the constant comparison that platforms such as Instagram and Facebook invite.

4.3. Psychological Factors

Delving into psychological underpinnings, we find that our mindset, thoughts, belief systems, and coping mechanisms significantly influence our anxiety levels. The Cognitive Model of Anxiety illustrates how our thoughts cause our feelings and behavior—not external things like people, situations, or events. So, if our thoughts are skewed towards perceiving more danger, fear, or worry, these will translate into feelings of anxiety.

Particular styles of thinking, such as catastrophizing (worst-case thinking), black and white thinking, or rumination (persistent overthinking), contribute to anxiety. An individual's self-perception and self-esteem also play decisive roles. Anxiety often tends to be higher among individuals dealing with low self-esteem and negative self-perception.

The truth about human experience is that it is not linear or singular. The roots of anxiety are intricate and intertwined. Understanding these roots allows us to foster empathy for our own, and others', experiences with anxiety. This underlying comprehension is the foundational brick in the wall of managing and overcoming anxiety. Equipped with this awareness, you can begin to tailor your personal road to recovery or assist someone you care about on their journey. There is immense power in knowledge, and understanding anxiety is the first step in reclaiming control over our lives.

Chapter 5. The Science of Anxiety: A Closer Look

To fully appreciate our quest to conquer anxiety, it's pivotal to understand the scientific premise behind the feeling of apprehension. Often, individuals experience anxiety as an abstract, all-pervading force. However, it's crucial to remember that anxiety has its roots deeply embedded in the neuro-scientific realm, which we'll now explore.

5.1. The Brain and Anxiety

Our brains are intricate networks of neurons, performing a ceaseless classical concert of electrical and chemical messages. Comprehending anxiety requires us to delve into these subtle harmonics. Two areas of focus emerge here - the amygdala and the hippocampus.

The amygdala is the brain's alarm system, triggering anxiety and fear responses. Whenever you sense danger or stress, the amygdala activates, triggering physical reactions like increased heart rate or rapid breathing. On the other hand, the hippocampus is charged with processing traumatic memories, recollections that often spark off anxiety.

So how does this work? Imagine you're hiking and come across a snake. Your amygdala sets off the alarm, pumping adrenaline and causing you to jump back. Your hippocampus, on the other hand, files this event as a 'danger memory.' The next time you encounter a similar situation, these two regions synchronize to elicit an almost instantaneous anxiety or fear response.

Sometimes, however, these areas overreact to non-threatening situations, leading to what we understand as anxiety disorders.

5.2. The Neurotransmitters

Neurotransmitters, often termed as the body's chemical messengers, also play a crucial role in anxiety. Three prime players in managing our mood and anxiety levels are serotonin, norepinephrine, and gamma-aminobutyric acid (GABA).

Serotonin, often referred to as the 'feel-good' neurotransmitter, helps regulate mood, ensure restful sleep, and balance appetite. Lower serotonin levels are typically associated with depression and anxiety.

Norepinephrine deals with stress responses and arousal. It gears the body for a 'fight or flight' situation by raising heart rate and pumping glucose into your bloodstream. Its imbalance, however, can lead to anxiety or mood disorders.

GABA, on the other hand, inhibits or slows down brain signals, producing a calming effect. Lower levels of GABA have been found in people with anxiety and mood disorders.

5.3. The Role of Genetics

Studies have confirmed a genetic component to anxiety, suggesting people may be predisposed to these disorders via their genetic constitution. Multiple genes rather than one single gene are likely involved, each contributing a small fraction towards an individual's likelihood of developing an anxiety disorder.

Environmental factors, too, are crucial. Growing up in highly stressful situations or traumatic incidents can trigger anxiety disorders in individuals predisposed to them due to their genetic makeup.

5.4. Understanding Anxiety Disorders

The scientific understanding of anxiety disorders revolves around the interaction of our biology, environment, and personal history. Generalized Anxiety Disorder (GAD), Panic Disorder, Social Anxiety Disorder (SAD), and Post-Traumatic Stress Disorder (PTSD) are some examples of conditions falling under this category.

Each disorder has a distinct set of symptoms but shares commonalities rooted in constant fear or worry. Today, diagnosing these disorders relies heavily on a combination of behavioral assessments, self-reports, and clinician observations. Future efforts aim to integrate genetic and neuroimaging data to enhance diagnostic accuracy and therapeutic efficacy.

5.5. The Treatment Paradigm

The approach to treating anxiety, from a neurobiological perspective, primarily includes medications and talk therapy (psychotherapy).

Selecting the appropriate medication depends significantly on the nature and severity of symptoms. Some medications work by affecting neurotransmitters, while others address the physical symptoms of anxiety.

Psychotherapy, which includes Cognitive Behaviour Therapy (CBT) and Exposure Therapy, is considered highly effective, helping reframe thinking patterns, and confront and reduce fears.

In the quest to conquer anxiety, understanding these scientific aspects can solidify our path to recovery. By recognizing anxiety for what it is- tangible, comprehensible, and most importantly, beatable- we can equip ourselves better to outwit it. This exploration is the first step in regaining control and embracing the potential for an anxiety-free life.

Understanding the science of anxiety won't make it instantly evaporate. Still, it will help you gain a holistic view, demystifying it from an unapproachable dark cloud to a manageable opponent. And that, in itself, is an empowering place to commence your journey.

Chapter 6. Anxiety and Lifestyle: The Hidden Connection

A great deal of research has linked anxiety to lifestyle. Unhealthy lifestyle patterns can pave the way for anxiety and make its symptoms much more severe. Here are some ways lifestyle may intrinsically link to anxiety.

6.1. The Role of Diet

It's often said, "We are what we eat," and indeed, the quality of our food has great bearing on our mental health. Clinical Nutritionist, Dr. Josh Axe, asserts that an unhealthy diet may increase the risk of developing anxiety disorders.

Consuming highly processed foods high in sugar and low in nutrients can exacerbate anxiety symptoms. Sugar spikes and crashes can cause mood swings, triggering symptoms of anxiety. Likewise, certain food additives like aspartame can promote feelings of anxiety and panic.

Experts advise adopting a balanced diet high in fruits, vegetables, lean proteins, and whole grains, which can help manage anxiety. Certain foods even have calming properties. For example, foods rich in omega-3 fatty acids, like salmon and chia seeds, promote brain health and alleviate anxiety symptoms.

Moreover, studies point to the gut-brain axis, the bidirectional communication between the digestive tract and the brain. A healthy gut promotes a healthy mind, reinforcing the importance of a balanced, nutritious diet. This principle forms the basis of psychobiotics, where certain types of bacteria (probiotics) in your gut positively influence your mood.

6.2. Sleep and Anxiety

The correlation between sleep deprivation and anxiety is a two-way street. Anxiety might rob you of sleep, or a lack of sleep can exacerbate anxiety symptoms. A study published in the Journal of Behavior Therapy and Experimental Psychiatry found that people who didn't get quality sleep were more likely to suffer from an anxiety disorder.

Establishing healthy sleep hygiene is integral to managing anxiety. Going to bed and waking up at the same time every day, avoiding caffeine and screens before bedtime, and creating a comfortable sleeping environment can all improve sleep quality, managing anxiety in turn.

6.3. Physical Activity and Anxiety

Physical activity is universally accepted as a non-pharmacological intervention for managing anxiety. Engaging in regular exercise releases endorphins—the body's natural 'feel-good' hormones, improves mood, aids in sleep, and provides a natural distraction from anxious thoughts.

Fitness and health expert, Jillian Michaels, suggests maintaining a regular exercise regimen, incorporating both aerobic activity such as running or swimming and strength training for comprehensive benefits. Exercise needn't be grueling to provide stress relief; even light activities like walking or yoga can help reduce anxiety symptoms.

6.4. Stress Management

A certain degree of stress is common as we navigate life's hurdles. However, chronic stress without proper management can lead to anxiety disorders. Hence, stress management forms an integral part of lifestyle changes necessary to combat anxiety.

Mindfulness-based stress reduction (MBSR) practices like meditation and deep breathing exercises can fortify resilience against stress. Similarly, relaxing activities like reading, listening to music, indulging in hobbies can buffer against stress.

6.5. Social Interactions and Anxiety

Social connections are crucial for mental health. Loneliness or isolation can lead to or worsen anxiety. Conversely, supportive, positive relationships can contribute significantly to anxiety management.

Dr. Julianne Holt-Lunstad, a psychology professor, emphasizes the role of strong social ties in reducing anxiety and improving overall mental health. Joining community groups, volunteering, or seeking the company of supportive friends can alleviate feelings of loneliness and anxiety.

Furthermore, for some individuals, reducing or limiting interaction with toxic or negative influences can also significantly reduce anxiety symptoms.

6.6. The Impact of Substance Use

Substance use, such as excess caffeine, alcohol, nicotine, or illicit drugs, can trigger or aggravate anxiety. Certain substances initially provide a false sense of calm or escapism, only to heighten anxiety in the long run.

Dr. Daniel K. Hall-Flavin of Mayo Clinic advises gradually reducing caffeine and alcohol intake. He suggests completely avoiding illicit substance use to manage anxiety. If substance dependence is an issue, professionals can provide necessary help.

6.7. Conclusion

The intricate relationship between anxiety and lifestyle subtly impacts our mental well-being. Understanding and modifying various lifestyle factors can significantly help in managing anxiety. This not only includes a balanced diet, exercise, and sound sleep schedule, but also a nurturing social environment, effective stress management, and avoiding harmful substances.

Still, it's important to remember that lifestyle changes are not a cure-all solution. Sometimes, medical treatment is crucial, especially in case of severe anxiety. However, incorporating these changes can serve as a supportive measure and help in the overall anxiety management strategy. In fact, the beauty of these strategies lies in their convergence: they not only help combat anxiety but also promote overall mental and physical health.

Chapter 7. Recognizing Anxiety Triggers: Your Personal Catalogue

Recognition is the first step towards intervention. To conquer anxiety, you must first understand its roots and learn to identify the triggers that spark these uncomfortable bouts of anxiety. This chapter aims to function as a guide, carefully mapping out the process to help you recognize and understand your personal anxiety triggers, and hence, equip you with the tools to regain control over your life.

7.1. Understanding Anxiety Triggers

Anxiety triggers are specific stimuli that bring about a rush of anxious feelings and thoughts. These triggers can range from certain people, places, and situations to more personal and internal triggers such as specific thoughts or emotions. Remember, what may trigger anxiety in one person may have no effect on another, indicating the personalized nature of this condition.

7.2. Identifying Personal Triggers

Overcoming anxiety begins with identifying the triggers peculiar to you. Below we touch upon various potential triggers that are typically associated with sparking anxiety. These will assist you in discovering your anxiety's origin and helping you construct your personal catalogue of triggers.

- **People and Social Situations:** It could be certain people or social events that cause your anxiety to rise. Gatherings, meetings or even smaller encounters with particular individuals may trigger an anxiety attack.

- **Places:** Certain physical locations can also cause an increase in your anxiety levels. It may be a particular room, a public place, or a previously visited location tied to a stressful event.

- **Sights, Sounds, and Smells:** Sensory triggers can also contribute to the sudden onset of anxiety. A specific aroma, type of sound or visual element can bring back memories or feelings associated with anxiety.

- **Personal Circumstances and Life Events:** Major life changes, personal health issues, or family circumstances might create anxiety. This includes changes in employment, grief, or financial troubles.

- **Patterns of Thinking:** Overthinking, worrying, or other negative cognitive patterns also have a significant contribution to anxiety.

After identifying these trigger categories, keep a record of your anxious feelings and thoughts when they arise, along with what you were doing, who you were with, and where you were. Over time, you will start noticing patterns.

7.3. Constructing Your Personal Catalogue

Making a personal catalogue of your anxiety triggers can be extremely helpful in managing anxiety. Track your anxiety triggers and the details of the anxiety episodes. This record will serve as a reflective tool and aid your journey towards overcoming anxiety.

- **Document the Event:** Write down the circumstances leading up to and during the onset of anxiety. Try to capture every detail about your surroundings, the people, the conversations, and your thoughts at that time.

- **Rate Your Anxiety Level:** By rating your anxiety level on a scale of 1-10, you can begin to differentiate between triggers having a minor or more significant impact.

- **Record Your Physical Sensations:** Make a note of the physical changes you experienced such as increased heart rate, sweating, trembling, etc.

- **Identify the Outcome:** Write down how you managed the anxiety and what the outcome was. This will help you identify coping mechanisms that were successful, and those that were not.

By regularly updating this catalogue, you can start to uncover patterns in your triggers and the efficacy of your coping strategies.

7.4. Transforming Triggers Into Growth Opportunities

Once identified and understood, anxiety triggers can become a starting point for personal growth and transformation. Each trigger is an opportunity for self-exploration and action.

- **Cognitive-Behavioral Techniques:** Engaging in Cognitive-Behavioral Techniques can help change negative thought patterns that are creating or magnifying your anxiety.

- **Mindfulness and Relaxation Techniques:** Mindfulness can help ground you in the present moment, reducing the anxiety borne out of future worries or past events.

- **Building Resilience:** Seeing triggers as opportunities to grow can empower you towards building your resilience. Over time, dealing with triggers will become more manageable, and they may even lose their intensity.

To end, understanding and cataloguing your anxiety triggers is a powerful tool in restoring control over your life. Remember, this process takes time and patience. Celebrate your progress at each step, and remember, every step forward, no matter how small, brings you closer to a life where anxiety no longer holds the reins.

Chapter 8. Cognitive Behavioral Techniques: Rewiring Thoughts

Cognitive Behavioral Techniques (CBT) are at the forefront of proven approaches to manage and overcome anxiety. Individuals equip themselves with these tools to monitor and address thought patterns and behaviors that fuel anxiety. Let's dive into these rewiring techniques, exploring their core principles, applications, and how they help transform our reactions to anxious thoughts.

8.1. Understanding the Foundation of CBT

The essence of Cognitive Behavioral Techniques revolves around the interconnectedness of thoughts, emotions, and behaviors. Afterall, our thoughts influence our feelings, dictate our actions, and ultimately shape our reality. Some mental constructs or beliefs about ourselves and the world around us can trigger anxiety or stress. CBT equips individuals with the ability to identify and challenge these distorted thoughts, consequently fostering healthier emotions and behaviors.

Primarily, we have two types of thoughts - automatic thoughts that quickly cross our minds because of certain events and core beliefs that are ingrained within us from our experiences, upbringing or environment. Automatic thoughts pose less resistance as they change with events, however, core beliefs are tough nuts to crack. They've been part of us for so long that they begin to seem like absolute truths.

8.2. The Technique: Dissecting the Thought Process

To embark on the journey of CBT, it's pivotal to dissect our thoughts, to understand them rather than spiraling into them. It's more of an 'observational' role. Here's an example of how thought tracking should look:

1. Event: Your boss points out a mistake in your work.

2. Automatic Thought: "I can't do anything right."

3. Feeling: Discouragement and anxiety.

4. Behavior: Procrastination or avoidance of tasks.

Understanding this sequence is crucial as it helps you to step back and challenge the automatic thoughts that frequently engulf you.

8.3. Challenging Negative Thoughts

As the saying goes, "we can't stop the birds from flying over our heads, but we can certainly prevent them from building a nest." The basis of this strategy is challenging the legitimacy of our automatic thoughts.

Once you've picked upon an anxious thought, don't fight it; instead, question it. Ask yourself, "Is this thought accurate? Is it helpful?" Perhaps you'll find that often your thoughts are not as accurate as you assumed, and breaking these illusionary perceptions can significantly decrease the magnitude of anxiety.

8.4. Rewiring Through Rational Counter Thoughts

One practical and effective strategy of CBT is to come up with rational counter thoughts for each anxious thought. Doing this consistently aids in rewriting your thought patterns.

Here is an example:

Anxious thought: "Everyone at the party will judge my conversation skills." Rational counter thought: "Not everyone will be paying attention to each thing I say, and it's okay to make mistakes while speaking."

This arduous, yet rewarding process, ensures that you don't fall into the pit of negativity and start viewing yourself through the lens of compassion.

8.5. Exposure Therapy: An Integrative Approach

Sometimes our reactions to anxious thoughts or scenarios are avoiding them. Yet, as paradoxical as it may seem, embracing such circumstances can be healing. This leads us to discuss Exposure Therapy, a potent aspect of CBT that involves gradual exposure to anxiety-inducing scenarios, assisting in reducing fear over time.

Remember, it's not about rushing, but rather taking small yet consistent steps towards anxiety-inducing situations until they no longer trigger unease.

8.6. Mindfulness: Connecting with the Now

One more ally in our CBT arsenal is practicing mindfulness. Being present and non-judgmental about the present moment can incorporate a seismic shift in our perceptions. The more we dwell on past mistakes or future possibilities, the more the anxiety amplifies.

Through mindfulness, we aim to ground ourselves in the 'now.' The key is removing the judgment filter while observing our thoughts and feelings, reducing the energy supplied to the cycle of anxiety.

As we conclude, remember, while CBT techniques hold a prominent potential in curbing anxiety, everyone has a unique journey towards healing. Experiment, explore, and embark on these techniques at your pace. You are the sculptor of your thoughts, your behaviors, your life. Above all, be gentle on yourself throughout this transformational journey - battling a behemoth like anxiety isn't an overnight miracle, and that's perfectly alright.

Chapter 9. Mindfulness and Relaxation: Tools for Calm

Embracing mindfulness and relaxation techniques can profoundly influence how we perceive and manage anxiety. These mechanisms are not just about mitigating stress, but also enhancing our understanding of our thoughts, emotions, and overall self. This understanding enables us to cope with life more resourcefully.

9.1. The Artistry of Mindfulness

Mindfulness, a simple yet powerful technique, can be described as 'intentional, present-moment awareness without judgment.' This technique powers us to live in the present moment with full consciousness, embracing our experiences without labeling them as 'good' or 'bad.'

Practicing mindfulness entails dedicating time for just being and observing the experiences that emerge moment by moment. Through this method, we can cultivate a deeper awareness about our mental patterns, habitual reactions, and overall well-being.

One of the vital ways to practice mindfulness is through meditation. This method encourages us to sit quietly and focus on our thoughts, feelings, or sensations without judgment. Besides meditation, mindfulness can be practiced during routine activities such as eating, walking, or simply breathing.

9.2. Achieving Mindfulness through Meditation

Meditation helps us cultivate mindfulness by providing a medium to observe our thoughts and emotions without being entangled in them.

The practice involves concentrated focus on a particular object, thought, or activity to enhance awareness, attention, mental clarity, and calmness.

There are numerous ways to meditate. These include focus-based meditation (focusing on a particular object, phrase, or visualization), open-monitoring meditation (observing our thoughts and feelings openly without judgment), and mindfulness-based stress reduction (MBSR) techniques. You can identify the modality that suits you best and maintain a regular practice.

9.3. The Advantages of Mindfulness Meditation

Mindfulness meditation provides numerous psychological and physiological benefits. Psychologically, it enhances emotional regulation, reduces stress reactions, and promotes a sense of peace. Physiologically, it improves immune response, amends sleep quality, and upgrades flexibility towards stress.

Several research investigations have indicated that mindfulness techniques can nurture self-insight, morality, intuition, and fear modulation, all functions associated with the brain's middle prefrontal lobe area.

9.4. Experiencing Mindfulness in Everyday Life

Mindfulness is not just a concept useful in meditation but is a way of life and can be integrated into our daily routine. You can practice mindfulness while eating, drinking, communicating, or any moment where you can consciously pay attention to your sensory experience.

Try to integrate mindfulness into routine activities. When you are eating, direct all your attention to the taste, texture, and aroma of your food instead of multitasking. While communicating with others, practice active listening and avoid rushing to respond. In every situation, consciously choosing to direct your attention and awareness can mark the beginning of an enlightening journey of mindfulness.

9.5. The Power of Relaxation Techniques

The proponents of relaxation techniques believe that a better understanding and control over our physiological processes can help us counter stress and anxiety effectively. They educate the body to respond differently to anxiety, trigger relaxation responses, and break the vicious cycle of panic symptoms triggering fearful responses.

A few common relaxation techniques include deep abdominal breathing, progressive muscle relaxation, and visualization. Each of these techniques aims to evoke a different route to relaxation and peace.

9.6. Exploring Deep Breathing

Deep breathing is a straightforward relaxation technique that you can practice anywhere. It revolves around taking slow, deep, and measured breaths to facilitate relaxation.

Follow these steps for a Deep breathing exercise: Inhale deeply and slowly through your nose, allowing your chest and lower belly to rise as you fill your lungs. As you slowly exhale, let all the air out, expelling from the bottom of your lungs upward. Repeat this cycle for a few minutes.

9.7. Reveling in Progressive Muscle Relaxation

Progressive muscle relaxation (PMR) is a relaxation technique that includes tensing and then relaxing each muscle group. This method can aid you to understand the difference between tense and relaxed muscles and enable relaxation.

9.8. Harnessing the Power of Visualization

Visualization or guided imagery can take you on a mental vacation, with your imagination leading the way. In this relaxation technique, you create calming, peaceful visuals in your mind to relax and shift your focus away from stress and anxiety.

Remember, patience and regular practice are the key to mastering these techniques. In your conquest of anxiety, mindfulness and relaxation techniques act as powerful allies. By deliberately paying attention to the present moment without judgment, you bring about a shift in your consciousness. This shift helps shape your understanding, perceptions, and responses, aiding in regaining control of your experiences and life.

Rest assured, mastering such techniques do not happen overnight, but with persistent practice and commitment, conquering anxiety becomes achievable. Always remember, a calmer, more focused, and less anxious version of you is not a distant dream, but a reality that is now within your grasp.

Chapter 10. Healthful Habits: Nutrition and Exercise for Anxiety Reduction

In our pursuit to conquer anxiety, it is pivotal that we focus on the two fundamental pillars that sustain us — nutrition and exercise. Often, we overlook these elements while trying to tackle mental health issues, while they carry immense potential to mitigate the effects of stress and anxiety on our bodies and minds.

10.1. Nutrition's Role in Anxiety Management

Nutrition lays the foundation for our physical and mental wellness. It's common knowledge that our bodies require vitamins, minerals, and various nutrients to function optimally. However, it is equally important to realize that our brain – the command center for all our emotions, including anxiety – relies heavily on these nutrients for effective functioning.

When we consume a balanced diet rich in key nutrients, the brain gets equipped with the required fuel to produce neurotransmitters like serotonin and dopamine, which are essentially our 'feel-good' hormones. They help regulate our mood, sleep, and overall sense of well-being.

Let's examine certain foods and nutrients that play a significant role in anxiety management:

1. Omega-3 Fatty Acids: Known to promote brain health, omega-3s can lower anxiety levels and improve mood. Foods like fish (especially fatty fish like salmon, mackerel, and sardines), chia

seeds, flaxseeds, and walnuts are rich in these healthy fats.

2. B Vitamins: They are crucial for maintaining a healthy nervous system and aid in the production of our 'feel-good' hormones. Avail of the B-vitamin benefits from leafy greens, beans, peas, lean meats, eggs, and dairy products.

3. Magnesium: Often referred to as the 'relaxation mineral,' magnesium can help reduce anxiety symptoms. Incorporate magnesium-rich foods such as spinach, quinoa, almonds, cashews, and black beans in your diet.

4. Probiotics: Research suggests that a healthy gut can lead to a healthy mind, since a significant portion of serotonin is produced in the gut. Probiotics found in yoghurt, kefir, sauerkraut, and kimchi can support a healthy gut microbiome.

However, while focusing on what to add to our diet, we should not neglect what needs to be reduced or avoided. High sugar diets, caffeine, and alcohol can all exacerbate our anxiety.

10.2. Exercise: The Natural Antidepressant

Exercise is one of the most potent yet underutilized tools to combat anxiety. Regular physical activity not only enhances our physical well-being but also posits profound effects on our mental health.

Physical activity induces the release of endorphins, chemicals in the brain that act as natural painkillers and mood elevators. They bring about feelings of euphoria and general well-being. Consistent exercise leads to an increase in these endorphins, as well as serotonin and dopamine, thereby acting as a natural antidepressant.

The type of exercise doesn't have to be strenuous to be beneficial. Even simple activities like a brisk walk, yoga, swimming, or cycling can help. What matters is consistency.

Let's dive into the specifics of how different forms of exercise can aid in anxiety reduction:

1. Aerobic Exercises: Research indicates that regular aerobic exercise can decrease overall levels of tension, elevate and stabilize mood, improve sleep, and boost self-esteem. Even five minutes of aerobic exercise can stimulate anti-anxiety effects.

2. Strength Training: It works on the principle of applying stress to the muscles, and the body adapting to this over time. This principle not only makes the body more robust physically but also mentally by teaching the mind to adapt to stress.

3. Yoga: A mind-body practice known for its ability to reduce stress and promote relaxation. It brings together physical and mental disciplines to achieve a peaceful balance between body and mind.

In conclusion, while nutrition provides the right fuel to maintain mental health, exercise acts as a potent tool to mitigate anxiety and stabilize emotions. As we pay heed to these two essential components, they can significantly bolster our journey towards conquering anxiety.

Remember, introducing changes in diet and exercise patterns requires patience and perseverance. Set attainable goals, celebrate small victories, and gradually, these healthful habits will anchor you in your voyage to alleviate anxiety and affirm optimal mental wellness.

Chapter 11. Building Resilience: Nurturing Your Mental Fortitude

In our endeavor to conquer anxiety, one critical area that requires focus is building resilience. This, essentially, involves nurturing our mental fortitude. Consider it akin to building a mental muscle; the more we exercise it, the stronger it becomes, and the better we become at wrestling the crippling effects of anxiety.

11.1. Understanding Resilience

Before delving deeper into building resilience, it's crucial to understand its essence. Resilience is the ability to effectively adapt whenever we encounter significant sources of stress, like a significant illness, a catastrophe, or a tragic event. It doesn't mean we avoid experiencing adversity or distress, but it equips us to manage challenges and bounce back quicker.

It's important to remember that resilience isn't about toughing it out alone or suppressing your feelings. It's about having the strength to acknowledge your emotions, confront your fears, and find ways to deal with them.

11.2. The Importance of Building Resilience

Building resilience not only helps you manage anxiety better but also fosters improved self-esteem, bolstered relationships, and heightened satisfaction in life. It empowers you to face your fears and still move ahead, transforming them from debilitating foes to constructive allies.

Research studies correlate high resilience levels with enhanced emotional well-being, reduced stress, and better overall health. Therefore, fostering resilience can prove to be an effective weapon in combating anxiety and achieving peace of mind.

11.3. Cultivating Positive Relationships

The path to resilience is seldom traversed solo; positive relationships form its cornerstone. Fostering supportive connections with family members, friends, coaches, or therapists enriches your ability to cope with stress and anxiety.

Nurture relationships that provide comfort and encouragement amid challenging times—ones that aid mental growth and build your resilience muscle. Participate in social activities, lend a helping hand to others, or join relevant support groups. Remember, a network of social support is an asset when it comes to developing resilience.

11.4. Embrace Self-Care

Resilience isn't all about mental fortitude; a certain degree of physical stamina is necessary too. Ensuring regular exercise, maintaining a healthy diet, and getting adequate sleep can impact your physical energy levels, which, in turn, helps bolster your emotional energy and resilience.

Moreover, mindfulness exercises like meditation, yoga, and breathing exercises can help lower anxiety levels and improve your capability to handle stress.

11.5. The Power of Positive Thinking

Groundbreaking research reveals that one's mind-set plays a monumental role in developing resilience. Embracing positivity and being optimistic generate a sense of self-efficacy, creating an environment conducive to resilience-building.

Start by practicing gratitude, focusing on your achievements rather than defeats. Envision a successful future and take steps towards realizing it. Above all, smile—remember that problems are temporary phases and not a lifelong sentence.

11.6. Developing Coping Skills

With enough practice, anyone can develop effective coping skills as part of their resilience-building journey. Cognitive-behavioral therapy (CBT) techniques, for instance, can help you challenge negative thought patterns and replace them with healthier beliefs.

Adopting strategies like journaling your thoughts, setting aside time for reflection, and learning stress management techniques are pivotal in developing robust coping skills. Over time, these learned skills contribute significantly to building resilience.

11.7. Prioritizing Self-Growth

Resilience isn't a static state. Like any other skill, it needs regular nurturing and development. Each challenge or adversity offers an opportunity for self-learning and growth, for cultivating adaptability, and turning setbacks into comebacks.

Consider adversity a teacher and seize the opportunity to learn. Embrace a growth mindset and persist in the face of obstacles. This growth-oriented approach is a crucial part of building resilience.

11.8. Self-Efficacy

A key facet to resilience is the belief in oneself. Understand your strengths, embrace your vulnerabilities, and nurture a robust faith in your capacity to overcome.

Having faith in your capabilities translates into a robust sense of agency—an integral part of resilience. So, believe in yourself and know that you can navigate through the rough tides of adversity.

The journey of fostering resilience doesn't occur overnight. It requires persistent effort, courage, and continual learning. It purposes a change in perspective, a positive outlook, and unwavering faith in oneself. By nurturing your mental fortitude, you take a significant stride in conquering anxiety, regaining control of your life, and stepping confidently into a future free of anxiety's shackles.

The echoes of a resilient spirit reverberated in the words of Japanese writer Haruki Murakami: "And once the storm is over, you won't remember how you made it through, how you managed to survive. You won't even be sure, whether the storm is over. But one thing is certain. When you come out of the storm, you won't be the same person who walked in. That's what this storm's all about."

And remember, each one of us has that spark of resilience within us. The key lies in cultivating it with patience, perseverance, and positivity. You have the power to combat anxiety and emerge stronger. Your journey towards building resilience and conquering anxiety is but a thought away—take the leap and begin today.

Chapter 12. Getting Back to Normal: Your Personal Roadmap to an Anxiety-Free Life

Anxiety, a product of the primal instinct of flight or fight, can be debilitating when it overstays its welcome, transforming routine chaos into a tempest. Welcome to your solution, a detailed map leading you to an anxiety-free life. Along this journey, you'll find personal narratives, expert counsel, and a plethora of proven techniques designed to help you regain control.

12.1. The Nature of Anxiety

To combat the beast, we first need to know it. Anxiety is an emotional response to perceived danger—an alarm system hardwired into our brains to prepare us for combat or flight. But when this alarm sounds relentlessly—without a genuine threat—it converts into an anxiety disorder. If you've experienced restless nights, heart racing like a drum to the beat of unseen dangers or fears, irrational worries that trail you like a persistent shadow, it's time to claim back control.

12.2. Acknowledge, Don't Suppress

Your first strategy to navigate around anxiety is to acknowledge your emotions. It may sound trivial on the surface, but acknowledgement is the first step of recovery. Suppressing anxiety only lets it simmer under the surface, waiting for a trigger to explode. Instead, honour your feelings, however unsettling they may be. Identify what's causing you stress, and why. This understanding paves the way for meaningful change towards an anxiety-free state.

12.3. Know Your Triggers

Recognizing patterns of worry and understanding what initiates them is fundamental. Make a diary of such events, jot down every time you feel anxious. It could be a person, situation, place, or even a memory. Unravelling these triggers could help you actively mitigate future episodes.

12.4. Anxious Thoughts are not Facts

Realizing anxious thoughts are not realities is difficult but essential. Anxiety has a cunning way of dressing up falsehoods into truths. When anxiety tells you you're not good enough, that you're in danger, or any other damaging narrative, understand this is anxiety speaking, not the reality.

12.5. Implement Effective Strategies—Mindfulness

The practice of mindfulness—staying present and grounded in your current experience—can be a powerful tool. When anxiety whirls you into a storm of past regrets or future fears, hold onto this moment—right here, right now. Observe without judgment, exist in the present and you'll soon notice your anxiety recede.

12.6. Harnessing the Power of Positive Affirmations

Positive affirmations are powerful sentences that you repeatedly tell yourself to foster positive changes in your life. Choose affirmations that speak to you—'I am in control,' 'I am getting stronger every day,'—play these on repeat in your mind, especially during bouts of anxiety.

12.7. Healthy Lifestyle Choices

Lifestyle can greatly influence anxiety. Ensuring regular physical exercise, adequate sleep, and balanced nutrition are key. Cut off caffeine, alcohol, and any other stimulants that potentially escalate anxiety. Ensure to make time for yourself, embrace activities that offer a sense of calm—reading, meditation, yoga, or simply being in nature.

12.8. Incorporating Professional Help

If your anxiety becomes overwhelming, seeking professional help is not a sign of weakness, but a strength. Therapies like Cognitive Behavioral Therapy (CBT) and Exposure Therapy have shown lasting benefits. Medication could be another option for some individuals if recommended by a health professional.

12.9. Staying Resilient through Setbacks

Recovery isn't a straight line—it entails peaks and troughs. You may have periods of heightened anxiety despite your best efforts. This takes us back to acknowledging—recognize these setback periods as part of recovery, and don't chastise yourself. Instead, lean on your support system and continue implementing your strategies.

12.10. Embrace Progress, Not Perfection

Lastly, shedding anxiety is not about achieving perfection—it's about progress. Recognize and celebrate small victories. Each moment you stood up to anxiety, every positive change, however tiny, is significant.

In conclusion, regaining control over anxiety relies on your understanding to acknowledge and address it. Embrace mindfulness, positive affirmations, maintain a healthy lifestyle, and don't shy away from professional help when necessary. Accept setbacks as part of the journey, and acknowledge every step forward you make towards an anxiety-free life. It's your journey; take it at your own pace. Welcome to an anxiety-free life, it starts today.